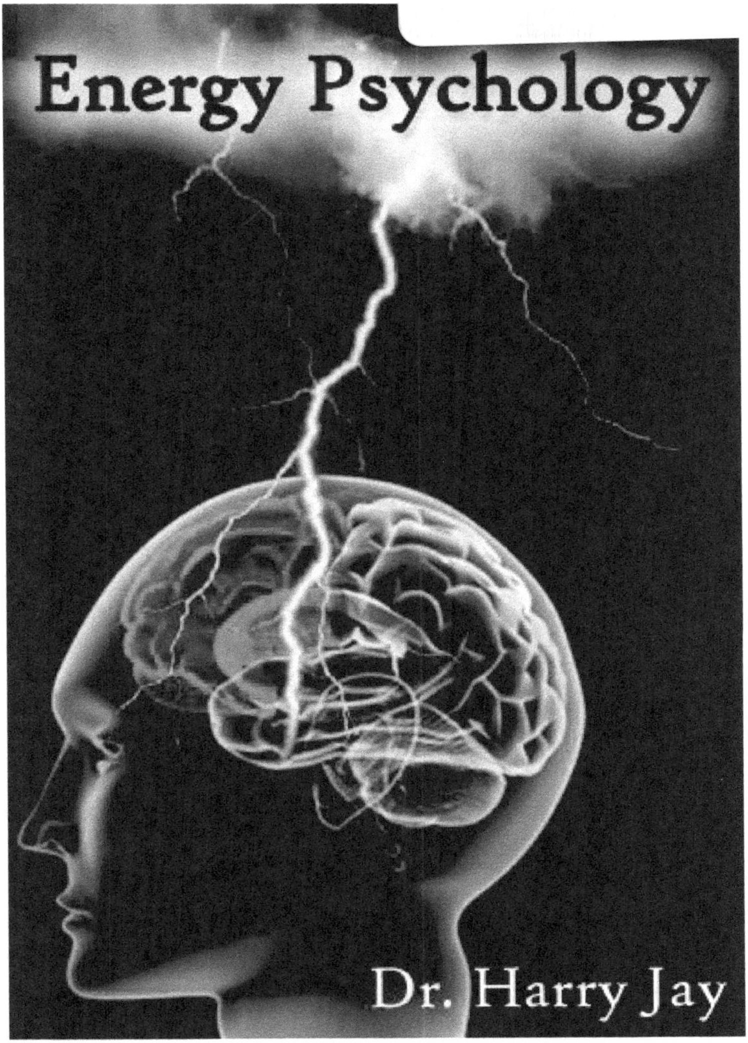

Energy Psychology

Dr. Harry Jay

Energy Psychology Techniques
©Copyright 2012 By Dr. Harry Jay

Introduction

The human mind can easily be considered the last great frontier. It is a vast, literally untapped resource and although we continue to research its riches; the more we learn, the more we realize what we do not know.

But knowledge is worthless unless it is applied. My goal is to introduce to my readers the knowledge we have gleamed through our extensive on-going research at Applied Mind Sciences in order to allow them to improve their lives.

Energy psychology involves many facets of research. It includes but is not limited to the "energy systems" that include the electrical activity of the nervous system and heart, biofields, meridians, biophotons and more and their relationship to the emotions, behavior, cognition and health. While psychological functioning includes thoughts, emotions, neurology chemistry, genetics as well as the environment, "bioenergy" is also involved.

The physical health of the body affects the mental health of the body and vice versa. It is important to remember that "everything is connected to everything" in the body.

Similar to the way a computer stores information in electromagnetic fields, our brains and body also function electromagnetically. Energy psychology can be applied to psychotherapy, physical health, pain management, sports and peak performance.

One of the better known methodologies is EFT. The corrective methodologies and protocols described herein are not "tapping" or other forms of "EFT" (emotional freedom technique) but rather newer research, the first has to do with removing pictures stored in the heart. EFT is a form of psychological acupressure, based on the same energy meridians used in traditional acupuncture to treat physical and emotional ailments for over five thousand years, but without the invasiveness of needles and has no similarity to the energy psychology techniques described herein.

This book describes corrective methodologies and protocols only that can be used to overcome and alleviate a variety of maladies. Protocols are treatment plans or procedures; modalities are considered the application of a therapeutic agent, usually a physical therapeutic agent.

Corrective Methodologies and Protocols Using Energy Psychology Techniques

Protocol #1: Removing Pictures of the Heart

The subconscious mind creates a belief system, which we call "pictures of the heart." These pictures involve either visions, or dreams/fantasies. Science has discovered that the subconscious mind cannot distinguish between fantasy and reality. This is the foundation of problems that occur within the human mind.

Perhaps the biggest problem people who are suffering from chronic emotional or physical disorders have is gaining access to a healing method that addresses the reason why the body and mind have failed to heal itself. Applied Mind Sciences solves that problem through bio-energetic testing, which can be done over the phone. It is totally unnecessary to see the patient in person. Applied Mind Sciences is therefore extremely accessible and it addresses the bio-energetic system where all the healing codes are stored and communicated to the body systems.

NOTE: Bio-energetic testing involves the use of medical machines such as an MRI to track and test the energy fields of the body. A lie detector machine is another example of bio-energetic testing that is outside the realm of medical testing.

"Many traditional therapies actually are treating symptoms rather than the underlying energetic dysfunction."

We believe people have a built-in homeodynamic mechanism to bring about and maintain healing – but sometimes this healing process becomes dysfunctional due to various forms of interference. The best form of healing is to remove whatever is hindering the body from healing itself and to give it access to its own healing mechanisms.

A Picture is Worth a Thousand Words

Envision a picture that conveys something beyond words. It may be a vacation picture at a place of incredible beauty. It may be a painful picture of a challenging time in your life. It may be a prized picture that exudes love and is a constant source of strength.

Recent brain research indicates that all data is encoded in the form of pictures (Owner's Manual for the Brain, by Pierce Howard, Ph.D.). In other words, pictures are the primary source that everything else flows from—they are the language of our lives.

A THOUSAND WORDS MAY BE NEEDED TO CONVEY A BELIEF, THOUGHT, OR FEELING.

Hypothetically, if we knew a person was going to develop a tumor in seven days, we might contract with a hospital to perform an experiment. The experiment is to perform a MRI daily, to pinpoint exactly when a person goes from being cancer-free, to having a tumor. Days one through six, the MRI reports a clear scan. On day seven, abnormal cells, representing a tumor, are seen.

QUESTION: Where did the tumor come from? The one place we know it did not come from is from physical things seen and measured by the MRI.

So, the tumor had to come from somewhere undetectable by the test.

Stanford researcher and cellular biologist, Bruce Lipton, Ph.D. released landmark research in 1998 that proves the unseen is the cause of the tumor in our example 95% of the time.

Dr. Lipton built upon Albert Einstein's e=mc2 (every problem is an energy problem) to scientifically prove the unseen cause of our hypothetical tumor. According to Dr. Lipton's research, the unseen cause is always a wrong belief.

In other words, a wrong belief creates a destructive energy frequency that manifests itself as disease, physical illness, mental or emotional disorder, stress, or one of a hundred other problems.

It sounds great, but there's something missing. Secular psychology, psychotherapy, spirituality, self-help, friendly and no-so-friendly advice…all have been touting, for hundreds of years, the secret to fixing the critical beliefs that dictate our health.

If these were THE problem, then fixing them would result in healing of the issue. Despite all these efforts, things are getting worse. According to the CDC, there is more heart disease than ever before. Everyone knows someone with cancer. Suicide rates are increasing, especially among teenagers and senior citizens.

Obesity is at epidemic proportions. Autoimmune disease has created the largest hopeless and helpless community in America. Mental health patients are weary of the treadmill of medication band-aids. The healthcare nightmare is a daily headline news story. WHY?

In recalling the pictures of your life, what feelings, thoughts, and beliefs are stirred? Did you experience anger and fear at recalling a major trauma? Pure joy in re-experiencing an innocent child playing on the beach? Affection at a first love's gaze? Inspiration, imagining life that is to come? Every feeling of sadness, anger, fear, or shame; every belief about yourself, others, and the world; every thought about the best course of action in a given situation—all of these exist because of, and are anchored to a picture.

A belief is an interpretation of something. A thought is a rational reasoning about something. A feeling is an experience of something. The picture is THE SOMETHING!

EACH BELIEF, THOUGHT, OR FEELING STIMULATES AN ENERGY SHIFT

Albert Einstein proved that all matter is controlled by energy ($e=mc^2$). All energy has a measurable frequency. In current medical technology, energy frequencies are measured with MRI's, CT scans, PET scans, EEG's, and others.

A current kidney stone removal therapy works by raising the frequency of the kidney stone, causing it to explode internally. Applied Mind Sciences treatments also use energy to heal the body. Applied Mind Sciences protocols heal the destructive pictures that are causing the wrong beliefs, which in turn, are causing the energy frequencies of illness and disease.

EVERY ENERGY SHIFT CAUSES A BIOCHEMICAL CELLULAR CHANGE

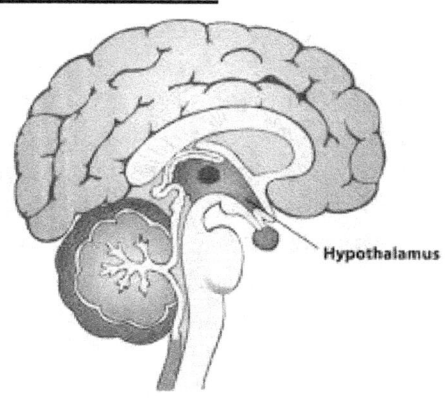

Hypothalamus

When the hypothalamus, in the brain, senses the energy frequency of fear, it activates the body's emergency response system and sends a signal to the pituitary, or master gland, that there is an emergency. The pituitary then sends a signal to the adrenal glands, which send out the adrenal hormone that puts the entire body into "fight or flight" mode.

"Fight or flight" is healthy when it allows the body to react to avoid a dangerous situation, and then returns it to rest. It is not healthy; however, for the body to activate "fight or flight," when the phone rings, and then remain in that state chronically.

When the body is chronically in a "fight or flight" place, healing resources are diverted from the major organs, the immune system, and higher neurological functioning. If the body stays in this state for an extended period, illness, disease, and disorder are likely to follow.

Dr. Lipton's research concludes that the energy frequency of fear and wrong beliefs will cause the nervous system to go into "fight or flight." Every wrong belief is an interpretation of fear pictures.

A NEGATIVE BIO-CHEMICAL CELLULAR CHANGE CAN RESULT IN ILLNESS, DISEASE, AND DISORDER

The above process that activates "fight or flight" can lead to a health crisis—one cell at a time. Dr. Lipton proved that every cell is either in growth mode or self-protection mode at any given time.

A cell in growth mode is healthy and impervious to disease. A cell in self-protect mode is closed to needed resources of the body and is vulnerable to dysfunction and disease. Cells switch from growth to self-protect mode when the HPA axis (fight or flight) is activated.

The HPA axis is wrongfully activated by the mistaken perception of danger. A destructive picture leading to a wrong belief always causes this mistaken perception of danger.

HEAL THE PICTURE, HEAL THE PROBLEM

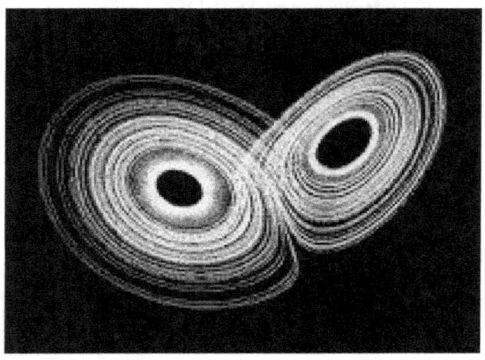

The homeodynamic mechanism of the body that, when activated, heals the destructive pictures of the heart. We know this is true because:

1. People report the picture or memory changing before their eyes.

2. People report that their sickness, disease, or disorder, is healing, as their pictures heal.

3. Unprecedented mainstream medical validation.

Heart Rate Variability (HRV) is a part of a category of elite diagnostic tests that show the exact state that the body is in at any given time.

Like MRI, HRV does not respond even one percent to placebo, according to 30 years of medical literature. Heart Rate Variability measures the exact state of the body's autonomic nervous system, which controls all of the automatic systems in the body.

In his most recent book, Dr. Roger Callahan reviews the 30 years of literature on HRV, and finds only two treatments that have ever been found to balance the autonomic nervous system. Both treatments took a minimum of six weeks and involved intensive exercise. Historically, Heart Rate Variability is not used to validate therapies because no treatment shows a short-term balancing of HRV.

Applied Mind Sciences self-treatment protocols almost always instantly balance the autonomic nervous system. In a recently completed four-year HRV study, Applied Mind Sciences self-treatments were found to balance, within 20 minutes, the autonomic nervous system as measured by HRV in 85% of cases (80% were still in balance 24 hours later).

After personally witnessing a demonstration of self-treatments, the director of a major HRV production company remarked, "What you are doing, according to 30 years of medical research, is impossible."

How Does Applied Mind Sciences do the Impossible?

Since the dawn of time, an unknown force has been causing and maintaining our wrong beliefs. Pierce Howard, Ph.D., in his recent book, The Owner's Manual for the Brain, cites research that concludes that all information is stored in the form of images.

These images are the real problem. It's almost impossible to heal any problem long-term without fixing the underlying picture.

If this picture is not healed, fixing the cell, belief, or feeling is usually a band-aid, allowing either the same problem to recur or a new problem to manifest.

HERE'S THE EVIDENCE:

- Of 2,000+ people who used self-treatment protocols as described, 99.5% healed completely or dramatically.

- No one who has done self-treatment protocols, as prescribed, has developed a major disease while doing it.

- Unprecedented in 30 years, HRV results show immediate balancing of the autonomic nervous system (previously believed to be impossible).

WHY IS THIS SO?

- According to Pierce Howard, Ph.D., (and many others) the picture is first.

- If you fix everything but the picture, you still have the problem.

- If you fix the picture, and nothing else, all of the problems heal.

HOW IS THIS SO?

The homeodynamic mechanism in the body fixes the destructive underlying pictures, quickly, effortlessly, and completely. This mechanism is the hidden fuse box in the body that heals the pictures when the correct switches are flipped.

Since this discovery, people from around the world, using Applied Mind Sciences self-treatment protocols, are fixing underlying pictures, which automatically heal wrong beliefs, which instantly heal destructive energies, which consistently heal: no medications, no surgery, no endless diet and exercise, no more self-help books, nothing to take, self-administered in your home.

The thing we hear from skeptics the most is, "That's too easy." It's not too easy; we've been making it too hard. This is the way it was always meant to be.

The Quantum Connection

Applied Mind Sciences unifies several established theories of physics and biology and adds a newly discovered and validated mechanism for healing. In 1993, David Bohm posited super quantum theory (quantum potential), theorizing that there is an unseen energy that pilots every cell and particle of the universe.

These pilots (Q) are beyond the fourth dimension geometry of space-time. Because Q acts beyond space-time, it can and does establish non-local connections. In other words, the super quantum of each cell is in instantaneous contact with all other super quantums (Undivided Universe, 1993).

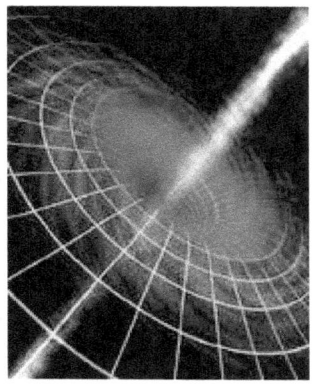

In 1994, the Einstein, Padowski, Rosen experiment was conducted. This landmark study and experiment was called, "The paradox in the brain: Transferred potential." In this experiment, two strangers were given a few minutes to get to know each other.

They were then separated into two electromagnetic cages 50 feet apart, where they were unable to see each other. Both participants were hooked up to neurological probes. They shined a penlight into one subject's eyes, which caused neurological activity to go crazy.

At the same instant, the other subject registered the exact same neurological activity, even though he was seemingly resting comfortably with no light in his eyes. The experiment was repeated at greater distances with the same results.

The conclusion of the experiment was that it didn't matter how far the subjects were separated—the super quantum transfer of information would still occur instantly.

In 1993, under the direction of the United States Army Intelligence and Security Command, white blood cells, leukocytes, scraped from the mouths of volunteers were centrifuged and placed in a test tube.

Probes from a recording polygraph, a lie or motion detector, were then inserted into the tube. The donor of the cheek cells was seated in a room separate from his donated cells and was shown a television program with many violent scenes.

When the volunteer watched scenes of fighting and killing, the probe from the polygraph detected extreme excitation in the mouth cells, even though they were in a room down the hall.

Subsequent repeats of the experiment showed the same results, with donor cells separated up to fifty miles and two days after donation. The donated cells remained energetically and non-locally connected with their donor and seemed to "remember" where they came from.

From The Heart's Code, by Paul Pearsall, Ph.D., Applied Mind Sciences discovered a mechanism in the body that allows the "Super Quantum" to be stimulated for the remote gathering of information, and to stimulate healing. It transfers the conscious intent of the person as an instruction to the "Super Quantum" pilot of each cell in the body, which then enacts a healing response in that cell.

Applied Mind Sciences coaches individuals so that they can treat themselves by healing wrong, destructive pictures that develop into beliefs. Recent research indicates that all incoming data to an individual is encoded in the form of pictures (Pierce Howard, Ph.D.,

The Owner's Manual for the Brain). The person then interprets these pictures. The interpretations become the wrong beliefs that, according to cellular biologist Bruce Lipton, cause energy and cellular shifts that cause all problems for the 95% of the population without genetic damage.

The self-treatment mechanisms that the client is coached in are a new and original system of hand placements and positions on the body. This system has yielded unprecedented results over the last four years in two areas:

(1) Clients' reports of healing, and

(2) Heart Rate Variability (HRV) pre- and post-tests. The Applied Mind Sciences self-treatment protocols take only 15 minutes.

Seven Secrets of the Human Mind

1. All information is stored as pictures.

2. All pre-language, trauma, and inherited pictures become the stimulus reaction system.

3. All stimulus reaction pictures are activated by similar events, actual or imagined.

4. Activation of stimulus reaction pictures causes re-experience of original pictures. Memories are only memories to the conscious; to the unconscious, they are current events.

5. The rational belief system is based on the stimulus reaction system.

6. When the head and heart conflict, the heart wins.

7. Activated heart pictures cause experience.

Healing Codes in the Voice

Assuming the body has all the required nutrients, we believe the mechanism to heal is made up of subtle energetic actions that communicate the healing data that interacts on body chemistry, body mechanics, and on the sense of emotional well-being.

Like a cellular telephone system, our mind-body functional communication system is partly hard-wired and partly dependent upon energized frequency fields that transmit coded data across unrelated space.

The transmission of the subtle energy information is passed through energy meridians. All languages are actually coded information, including the healing language of the body.

All actions of the body and mind require energy. Energy is defined as a force capacity to do a work. It can be in the form of potential (passively available) energy or kinetic (active) energy.

We are activating potential energies that are transformed into kinetic force releasing the healing data, which then restores the healing process.

Many of these codes can be revealed through a muscle-testing process but this is subject to rapid muscle fatigue and therefore impairs the completion of in-depth energy correction.

The quickest and most accurate method of revealing these bio-energetic codes has been by the voice. Global Reach' staff are highly trained and are able to discern healing codes and assessment data from the client's voice. In many cases relief is experienced immediately.

In other cases, there is a delay of minutes or hours while the body is processing. In a few cases, a person may have a healing response where he or she feels worse.

We have tested and re-tested these techniques over an extended period of time with hundreds of clients. Since implementing Applied Mind Sciences techniques, our results have skyrocketed and many of them are documented through Heart Rate Variability scans, blood tests, MRI's, and diagnostic bio-energetic machines.

These new techniques require absolutely no equipment, no muscle testing, and are not dependent on generic algorithms.

Each client gets tailor-made evaluation and remedy coaching as revealed by the client's own voice using Applied Mind Sciences techniques.

Heart Rate Variability Tests

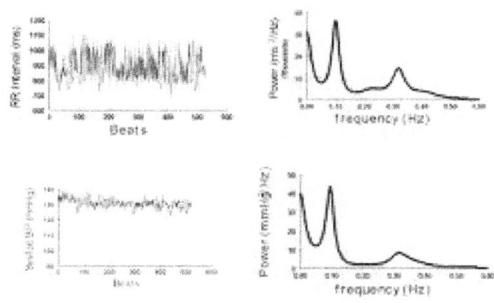

Three hundred clients were tested in the past four years using Heart Rate Variability (HRV) tests. HRV measures the intervals between heartbeats and is the best test in existence, according to 30 years of research, for measuring the degree of balance in the autonomic nervous system. HRV results are stable and unresponsive to placebo.

Applied Mind Sciences measured clients' HRV before determining a treatment. Then, Applied Mind Sciences identified the treatment and the clients immediately performed the treatment on themselves. Applied Mind Sciences then measured the client's HRV again.

Since 1998, Applied Mind Sciences achieved unprecedented results balancing the autonomic nervous system according to Heart Rate Variability (see Graph 1, next page).

Since developing Applied Mind Sciences protocols in 2000, the percentages of subjects still in balance after 24 hours increased tremendously (see graph 2, next page).

In his most recent book, Dr. Roger Callahan reviews the 30 years of literature on HRV, and finds only two treatments that have ever been found to balance the autonomic nervous system.

Both treatments took a minimum of six weeks and involved intensive exercise. Historically, Heart Rate Variability is not used to validate therapies because no treatment shows a short-term balancing of HRV.

Depressed HRV (defined in terms of the standard deviation of the means of all 'normal' intervals between two sequential beats without contained ectopic beats) has been shown to be associated with subsequent "cardiac events" such as angina, myocardial infarction, coronary heart disease, death, or congestive heart failure (Framingham Heart Study Group).

Low HRV may be a more powerful predictor of mortality than such standard determinants as left ventricular ejection fraction, wall motion abnormalities, frequency and complexity of ventricular ectopy, standard ECG indices, exercise capacity, and the signal averaged ECG (Fallen and Kamath, 1995).

Effect of Treatments as Measured by HRV Tests prior to development of protocols
214 Tests 1998-2001

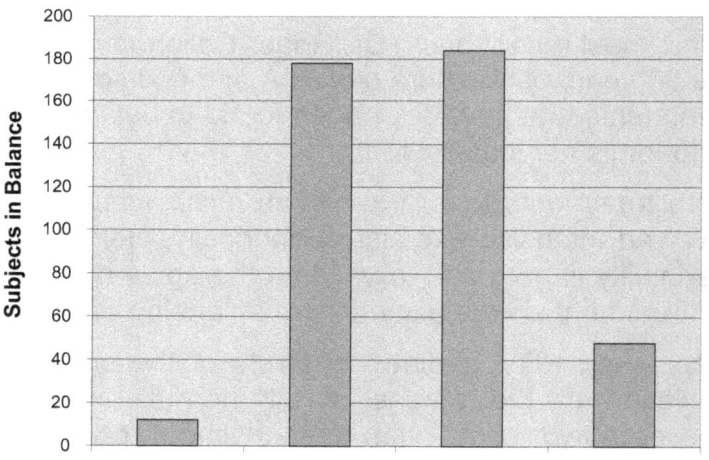

Energy Medicine

Sir Arthur Edington once said, "verily it is easier for a camel to pass through the eye of a needle than for a scientific man to pass through a door, and whether the door be a barn door or a church door, it might be wiser that he should consent to be an ordinary man and walk in rather than wait till all the difficulties involved in a really scientific method are resolved."

Albert Einstein stated, "It is possible that there exist human emanations that are still unknown to us. Do you remember how electrical currents and 'unseen waves' were laughed at? The knowledge about man is still in its infancy."

WHAT IS IT?

Energetic medicine, or bio-energetic consultation, is the practice of assessing and correcting health issues by way of the body's energy system, allowing the body's own immune system to do its normal healing work.

The body's energy system has been a fundamental part of traditional and alternative medicine for many, many years. An EEG measures the electrical activity of the brain in a similar way as the EKG measures electrical properties of the heart.

When the paddles are used to revive someone in cardiac arrest, it is with the accepted knowledge that the body and heart run on electricity. Over the past 50 years, the alternative health community has also effectively used various electrical methods, such as electronic acupuncture machines to assess various illnesses through the energy system of the person. In fact, without the use of the body's energy system for assessment purposes, modern traditional medicine would be set back 50 years or more.

Energetic medicine takes an additional step by using the energy system for correction purposes as well as for assessment.

WHY WORK WITH THE BODY'S ENERGY SYSTEM?

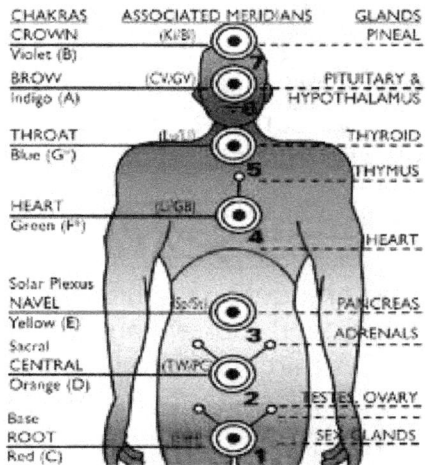

Atoms are made up of electrons, protons, and neutrons.

They are electrical particles. All herbs, vitamins, medications, and healing products are made up of atoms. Therefore, they are all electrical and each produces its own unique frequency. (Everything electrical MUST have an electrical frequency)!

Therefore, all healing of ANY kind involves energy. What's more, the energy seems to be the primary issue.

Every cell in our body MUST have energy or it dies, even if the tissue, bones, blood, and chemicals are all fine.

String Theory, (the newest hope for a unified theory of matter), states that everything (rocks, air, or body tissue) is made of tiny strings of energy, each with its own unique frequency.

Savely Yurkovsky, MD, founder of FCT stated that the energetic domain is the most fundamental in the regulation of homeostasis and is the true source of health and disease.

He notes that we cannot have disease without having first an energetic disturbance in the cells and organs, rendering the energy flow ineffective.

He further points out that there are three predominant regulating domains in the human body, all of which are energetic in nature:

1) Electromagnetic

2) Electric

3) Bio-Chemical

Every cell in the body has electromagnetic fields (EMF), electricity, and bio-chemical make-up. Electrical fields carry information data.

Each cell contains field data. Each thought field contains data.

There are data fields that are passed on through the generations through a phenomenon called isomorphic resonance.

In people, some energy forces are easily measured with instrumentation, while other energy fields are very subtle, requiring the body itself to be the resonant measuring instrument.

Bio-Energetic Testing

People have two options in health care. They can choose a modality that suppresses symptoms, or they can choose an intervention that seeks out the cause of the problem. In the latter method, the reason the immune system failed is addressed, allowing the body to heal itself as intended by the Creator.

The question is how do we assess the root of the problem? Most tests just identify and quantify the symptoms of the real problem.

The answer is found in bio-energetic testing, which identifies the body's stress reactions to various domains. Although Dr. Savely Yurkovsky uses a resonant bio-energetic testing method different than Global Reach, he states, "Bio-energetic testing is, in my opinion, the most sensitive single diagnostic tool that exists in the world today."

He further states:

I must tell, from my own personal experience, in reviewing the great body of literature that exists in the world today in various countries on the subject of bio-energetic testing, that when properly performed, it is far superior to any diagnostic modality that exists today in the world. It is far superior to any blood, laboratory, or imaging techniques in the sense of the depth of the penetration that these tests are capable of and able to register even minute deviation in bio-cellular fields that take place on the cellular,

sub-cellular, and intracellular structures, in my opinion, including the DNA.

One might have the correct combination of chemicals, vitamins, minerals, water, protein, carbohydrates, fats, etc., but none of these function properly when the information fields are disrupted because the hormones and enzymes are not recognized when the energy field information is energetically changed.

Dr. Yurkovsky points out, in his training that, "the normal energy flow in a person's body carries a primary role for his or her proper maintenance of physiology and homeostasis."

This has been taught for the last 5000 years in Chinese medicine, and is confirmed daily by the latest discoveries of science.

What Others Say

"All matter is energy field."

Albert Einstein (1879-1955)

"The Physician should look for the force and nature of illness at its source.

He is not to look to that which can be seen, for we are not called to extinguish the smoke, but the fire itself."

Theophrastus Paracelsus, M.D., Switzerland (1493-1541)

"Treating humans without concept of energy is treating dead matter."

Albert Szent-Gyorgyi, M.D., Hungary, Nobel Prize Laureate (1893-1986)

"Future medicine will be based on controlled energy fields."

Prof. William Tiller, Ph.D. (Stanford University)

"The energy field starts it all."

Prof. Harold Burr, Ph.D. (Yale University)

"The idea of a microbe as a primary cause of disease is the greatest scientific silliness of the age."

Pierre Antoine Bechamp, France (1816-1908)

"Diseases are to be diagnosed and prevented via energy field assessment."

George Crile Sr., M.D., Founder of the Cleveland Clinic (1864-1943)

"Body chemistry is governed by quantum cellular fields."

Prof. Murray Gell-Mann, Nobel Prize Laureate, USA

"All living organisms emit field."

Semyon D. Kirlian, U.S.S.R. (1900-1980)

All health issues follow energy like a row of dominoes follows the first domino.

When non-toxic and non-invasive corrections of the energy system are used to heal, the absolute bottom line root cause of the problem can be corrected - the first "domino."

When working with the body's energy system, one is simply removing barriers to the body – healing itself as it was designed to do with miraculous efficiency.

ALL HEALTH PROBLEMS have a toxic or aberrant frequency in the involved cells. A healthy liver cell has a different frequency than a diseased liver cell in the same person.

If the unhealthy frequency can be changed to a healthy frequency and maintained, the cell will heal and become a positive force to all surrounding cells.

THIS is the goal of energy medicine.

Energy MEDICINE vs. Traditional Medicine

Reductionistic (traditional) Medicine takes a complex set of components and reduces them to simple terms.

This leads to the development of a synthetic chemical reduced from a complex natural source, down to its key ingredients, with the hope of achieving pharmacological success.

In doing so, they rob the support structure built into the natural source.

One example is that of Valerianaccae, from which Valerian tea is made. This naturally occurring part of a plant has been used for thousands of years to induce sleep and decrease stress.

The reductionistic (traditional) medicine sought the key ingredient from the plant thereby, synthetically derived Valium.

Millions of people used Valium to relax muscles and reduce tension. Later a synthetic chemical derivative of Valium was used.

The development of the synthetic Valium resulted in side effects.

And society has had to deal with a significant number of Valium toxicity cases.

The synthetic reductionistic process, thought to be a solution, caused a significant social problem.

This process robs the Valerian tea of synergistic components such as vitamins, minerals, and trace elements needed to balance the naturally occurring reaction in the body.

Over 30 clinics have been established in America to deal with Valium addictions.

Valium toxicity has developed into one of the greatest chemically induced diseases known, and yet to date, around the world there is no Valerian tea clinics.

In fact there are no medical records of any Valerian tea toxicity or overdose.

In the same way, "Quantum" corrects health problems synergistically. The Applied Mind Sciences process simply seeks to identify and eliminate problems in the body's energy system that are preventing the body from healing itself as it was designed, by God, to do.

We receive all of our information from the body (not a standardized manual) and we do nothing invasive.

Reductionistic (traditional) methods seek to find the malfunction and force the desired symptom reduction. This is usually accomplished through cutting, burning, or poisoning.

An Unhealthy Trend

In 1986, one million people were dying of heart disease and 870,000 were getting cancer.

In 1993, one million were still dying of heart disease, and 1.2 million were getting cancer, of which 435,000 died from cancer alone.

In 1993, one million were still dying with heart disease, and 1.2 million were getting cancer, with 720,000 dying from cancer alone.

Taking the low average of the two years, 4,713 men, women, and children die every day with cancer or heart disease.

That is 141,390 persons every month on an ongoing basis.

This is equivalent to the destruction, in lives, of more than two atomic bombs every month, which are more than 24 atomic bombs every year in the United States alone.

As far as human casualties, this makes any war that we have ever had almost insignificant in comparison! AND IT IS GETTING WORSE EVERY YEAR!

Why is this happening?

Individuals today have over five hundred different insecticides and herbicides in their cells.

There is five times more DDT in the cells of every person in America than what we thought was safe ten years ago.

There is over ten times more strontium 90 in the bones of every person in America than what was considered safe ten years ago.

Environmental toxicity is now becoming a new area of study due to its pervasiveness in the world today.

Petro-chemical toxins, vinyl plastic toxins, heavy metal toxins and the like put the body under more bio-chemical stress than was thought to be survivable in the recent past.

Today many sufferers of environmental illness are written off as psychological cases and their suffering is discounted in traditional medicine.

We believe these sufferers of environmental illness are the "canaries" of our society. In olden days, miners would keep canaries in the tunnels to warn them when the air was toxic.

The birds would die first, giving the miners a chance to escape with their lives. Today those individuals with environmental illness are indicating that our environment is becoming too toxic for us to live in and remain healthy unless we take steps to safe guard our energy systems.

Mainstream medicine has a more narrow focus because it is based upon reductionistic Newtonian thought, looking for one cause of disease.

Stress, pathogens, trauma, and toxicity present a complex set of variables combining to cause disease.

Many diseases are not the result of just one factor, but often are a dysfunction of the body as the result of multiple variables affecting the body.

The new science of Energetic Medicine is based on chaos, wholeness, and fractal mathematics - all manifesting first in the body's energy system.

This therapy operates with the approach of balancing the body as a whole, chemically and energetically.

Recent research indicates that energy medicine is the fastest growing area within the entire health field, and among the fastest growing professions in all fields.

There is only one reason for this - IT WORKS! Applied Mind Sciences is a brand new modality in the exciting field of Energy Medicine.

It addresses the energetic cause of the dysfunction. Applied Mind Sciences is fast, effective and non-invasive. In the long run it is much more cost effective than modalities that never address the root cause.

Conscious Conflict

Some people report that their healing is not as quick as they expected.

One reason may be what we call conscious conflict.

Conscious conflict can be defined as a behavior or set of circumstances in your life, which violates your belief system over which you have control. In psychology we call it cognitive dissonance.

An example of conscious conflict is cheating on your taxes, or taking pens home from work. You know it's wrong, but you do it anyway.

Another example of conscious conflict might be if you know your spouse or child is lying to you.

Obviously, you don't have control over their behavior, but you do have control over whether or not you ignore their behavior or speak up against it.

We all have unconscious conflict in our lives.

This type of conflict is not harmful to the healing process because we need to be conscious of something before we can do anything about it.

Some people even report that as they do the protocols, they become more aware of conflict in their lives.

At this point, we need to take inventory and determine if there is something in our lives that violates our belief system over which we have control.

SAMPLE PROTOCOL: BALANCING THE AUTONOMIC NERVOUS SYSTEM

INSTRUCTIONS: Throughout each protocol session, focus alternately on a Love Picture; imagine yourself surrounded by people you love and people who love you, including God, if that fits your belief system.

Follow each of these steps:

- ☐ Complete the following Autonomic nervous system Protocol for the specified number of minutes and specified times per day.

- ☐ Complete the Booster Protocol (*after completing the Autonomic nervous system Protocol*) for the specified number of minutes and specified times per day.

- ☐ Continue the Autonomic nervous system Protocol and Booster Protocol for as long as necessary until the intensity of either the Early Picture or Current Picture you are focusing on reaches zero (0).

☐ Consider your autonomic nervous system issue. If it is resolved, move to using just the Autonomic nervous system Protocol Maintenance every day.

Balancing Autonomic Nervous System Protocol

On your nose, place your LH

On your forehead, place the back of your RH

2 minutes

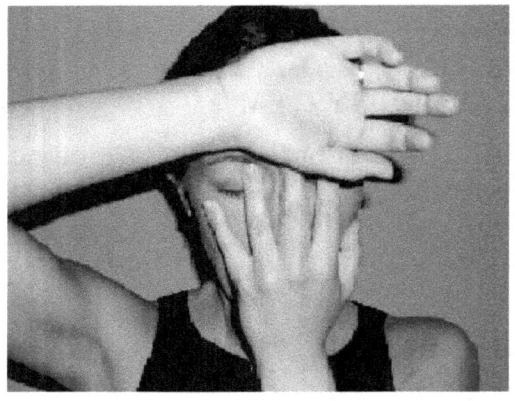

On the front of your neck, place your LH

Thumbnail

Index finger nail

Little finger print

On your forehead, place the back of your RH

1 minute

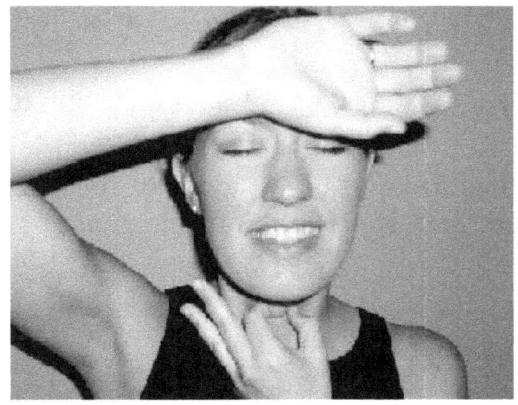

Synergy Package

1 minute

2 times/day

(5-times/day maximum)

Autonomic Nervous System Protocol Maintenance

<u>**Once your issue is resolved**</u>, it is important to continue using the protocols daily for maintenance.

Daily work is critical to keep the autonomic nervous system in balance, and to prevent the return of your issue.

On your nose, place your LH. On your forehead, place the back of your RH, 1 minute

On the front of your neck, place your LH Thumbnail, Index finger nail, Little finger print

On your forehead, place the back of your RH. ½ minute

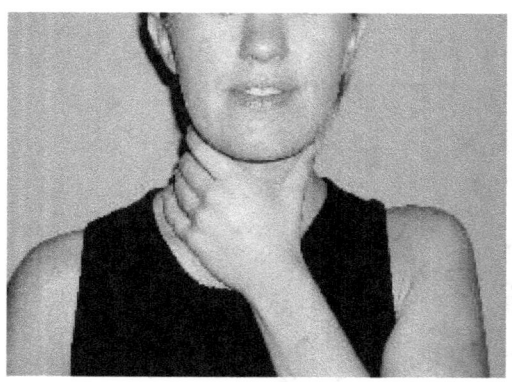

Synergy Package: ½ minute, 2 times/day, (5-times/day maximum)

BOOSTER PROTOCOL

On the front of your neck, place your whole LH

On the back of your neck, place your RH

Thumbprint

Middle finger nail

Ring finger nail

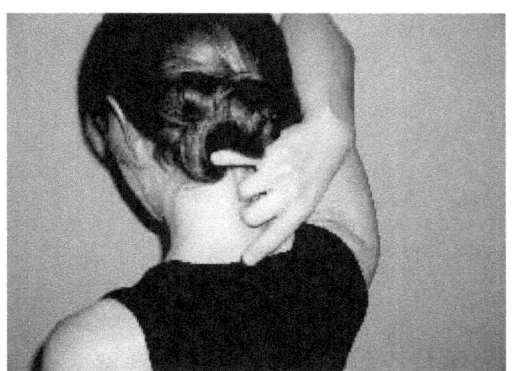

3 minutes

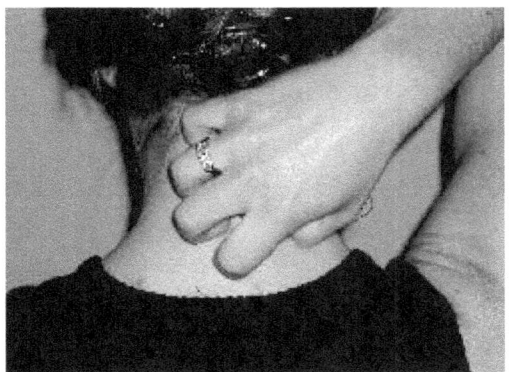

On the back of your neck, place all of your RH nails

On the front of your neck, place your LH

Thumbnail

Middle finger nail

Little finger nail

2 minutes

2 times/day

(4-times/day maximum)

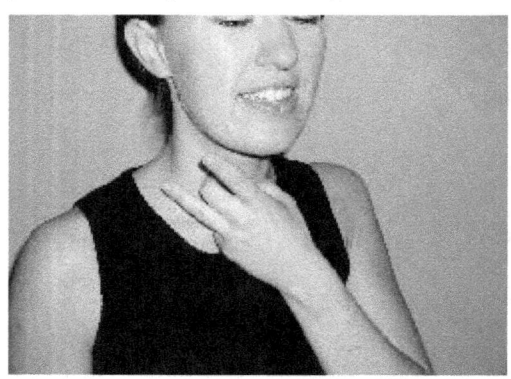

Energy Psychology Techniques is a book that is truly an amazing compendium of the latest research techniques and protocols related to the field of Energy Psychology.

The results are nothing short of stunning. See the special offer below…

<u>Self-Treatment Protocols:</u> You really can treat yourself using your body's energy.

The techniques offered are simple to put into effect with photos and complete instructions.

Why suffer when you can get the relief you need to live a high-quality of life.

Below is a list of protocols designed to work with certain symptoms and maladies priced at $19.95 each.

Write to us at mailto:support@epubwealth.com to purchase. One of our staff behavioral scientists will explain the protocol and monitor your progress.

- Abandonment-Rejection
- Abuse
- Acid Reflux
- ADD-ADHD
- Addiction
- Allergy
- Amouraphobia
- Anger
- Anxiety
- Arthritis

- Autonomic Nervous System
- Bedwetting
- Booster Protocol
- Carpal Tunnel
- Confidence
- Confusion
- Constipation
- Dental
- Depression
- Eating Disorder
- Emotional Bipolar
- Emotional Crisis
- Energetic
- Magnetic Frequency
- Energy
- Eyesight
- Fears
- Forgiveness
- Frustration
- Genetic Diseases
- Grief-Loss
- Guilt
- Headache

- Hearing
- High Blood Pressure
- High Cholesterol
- Impotence
- Irrational Thinking
- Jet Lag
- Menstrual
- Obsessive-Compulsive
- Overwhelmed
- Pain
- Peak Performance
- Phobia
- Preventative
- Sadness
- Shame-Guilt
- Sickness
- Sleep Problems
- Stress
- Upset Stomach
- Weight

I Have a Special Gift for My Readers

I appreciate my readers for without them I am just another struggling author attempting to make ends meet.

My readers and I have in common a passion for the written word as well as the desire to learn and grow from books.

My special offer to you is a massive ebook library that I have compiled over the years. It contains hundreds of fiction and non-fiction ebooks in Adobe Acrobat PDF format as well as the Greek classics and old literary classics too.

In fact, this library is so massive to completely download the entire library will require over 5 GBs open on your desktop.

Use the link below and scan all of the ebooks in the library. You can select the ebooks you want individually or download the entire library.

The link below does not expire after a given time period so you are free to return for more books rather than clog your desktop. And feel free to give the link to your friends who enjoy reading too.

I thank you for reading my book and hope if you are pleased that you will leave me an honest review so that I can improve my work and or write books that appeal to your interests.

Okay, here is the link…

http://tinyurl.com/special-readers-promo

PS: If you wish to reach me personally for any reason you may simply write to mailto:support@epubwealth.com.

I answer all of my emails so rest assured I will respond.

Meet the Author

Dr. Harry Jay is Director of Research for Applied Mind Sciences, a mental health and mind research group, and is the author of over 100 books and research papers spanning his 31-year career as a behavioral scientist. He resides in Southern Utah and enjoys the outdoors, fishing and photography.

http://www.amazon.com/author/harryjay

Visit some of his websites

http://appliedmindsciences.com/

http://appliedwebinfo.com/
http://embarrassingproblemsfix.com/
http://www.epubwealth.com/
http://forensicsnation.com/
http://www.freebiesnation.com/
http://neternatives.com/
http://privacynations.com/
http://survivalnations.com/
http://thebentonkitchen.com
http://theolegions.org

Some Other Books You May Enjoy From epubWealth.com

21st Century Marketing Genius
http://www.amazon.com/dp/B008A07WBW
Addictions
http://www.amazon.com/dp/B006IGHQD4
Anatomy of Anxiety
http://www.amazon.com/dp/B00777QQYS
Applied Income Model
http://www.amazon.com/dp/B006WZN8M4
Applied Mind Sciences
http://www.amazon.com/dp/B007GK4U08
AWeber Primer
http://www.amazon.com/dp/B00A8G2E3M
A Woman Surrounds A Man
http://www.amazon.com/dp/B008DY2VDO
Be A Prepper
http://www.amazon.com/dp/B007IL5OE6
Be Prepared to Survive
http://www.amazon.com/dp/B007KJ0ANQ
BlueprintCashPro

http://www.amazon.com/dp/B006X0UASS
Blame Me Not
http://www.amazon.com/dp/B008D37AI6
Body Language
http://www.amazon.com/dp/B006INI18G
Body Talk
http://www.amazon.com/dp/B0079MA1XS
Bully America
http://www.amazon.com/dp/B008EJ6102
Cartoon Psychology
http://www.amazon.com/dp/B006IUHMN4
CashCodePro
http://www.amazon.com/dp/B006WZRCVM
Chasing Shadows
http://www.amazon.com/dp/B008A5ZRW8
Chelation Therapy
http://www.amazon.com/dp/B006J7YZ54
Confessions of a Child Predator
http://www.amazon.com/dp/B007BB97KU
Confessions of a Satanic Worshipper
http://www.amazon.com/dp//B007DR4838
Control Your Dreams
http://www.amazon.com/dp/B0071YN3L6
Cyber-Daters Beware
http://www.amazon.com/dp/B006J9T4NA
Distraction Marketing
http://www.amazon.com/dp/B006IUVBWM
Dropping Off The Grid
http://www.amazon.com/dp/B006JLGKLC
Drop Three Dress Sizes in 30-Days
http://www.amazon.com/dp/B007F7VHZI
Effective Email Advertising
http://www.amazon.com/dp/B006IV2300

Embarrassing Problems Fix - General Problems Vol 1
http://www.amazon.com/dp/B0075LOK3U
Embarrassing Problems Fix - Female Problems Vol 2
http://www.amazon.com/dp/B0075LO7AQ
Embarrassing Problems Fix - Male Problems Vol 3
http://www.amazon.com/dp/B0075LQNF8
Energy Psychology
http://www.amazon.com/dp/B006JOZ7G8
Famous Cartoon Quotations
http://www.amazon.com/dp/B007POZKNQ
Famous Quotations
http://www.amazon.com/dp/B007IRKDM8
Female Wolf Packs
http://www.amazon.com/dp/B006JMHD80
ForensicsNation Bushwhacker Program
http://www.amazon.com/dp/B007I9AHVS
ForensicsNationsStore.com Catalog
http://ForensicsNationStore.com
FreebiesNation Blueprint Program
http://www.amazon.com/dp/B007IFRQ9S
Gender Differences in Advertising
http://www.amazon.com/dp/B006IOCG9U
Howdie Doodie
http://www.amazon.com/dp/B00770WQXA
If It Is Broke; Fix It
http://www.amazon.com/dp/B006JM6NHM
I Have a Mind to Believe
http://www.amazon.com/dp/B006ITGY84
I Know I Am But Who Are You
http://www.amazon.com/dp/B006IOQL7I

In-Image Ads Marketing
http://www.amazon.com/dp/B006X03NBE
Interesting Facts About Left-Handed People
http://www.amazon.com/dp/B00744PXCA
Investment Phrases
http://www.amazon.com/dp/B008LO3Y00
It's All About Database
http://www.amazon.com/dp/B006JO0RBI
Latin Phrases
http://www.amazon.com/dp/B006ITY7TW
Legal Phrases
http://www.amazon.com/dp/B008LOA0Q6
Living Alone
http://www.amazon.com/dp/B0086O1ZC4
Love is the Way
http://www.amazon.com/dp/B006IVYPFG
Male-Female Realities
http://www.amazon.com/dp/B006ITYUNK
Man Up - The Decline and Fall of Manhood
http://www.amazon.com/dp/B006JA2UMG
Massive Traffic Generator
http://www.amazon.com/dp/B006IV1YRS
Men & Women…attract or attack
http://www.amazon.com/dp/B006IU8LU2
Mobile Commerce Blueprint
http://www.amazon.com/dp/B006JO1CX0
Mobile Text Voting
http://www.amazon.com/dp/B006JOI4ZO
Pay Per Call Marketing
http://www.amazon.com/dp/B006XVUD98
Pay Per View Advertising
http://www.amazon.com/dp/B006ZXMI4W
PhattyFat WheytLoss

http://www.amazon.com/dp/B0077902JW
PLR Cash Tactics
http://www.amazon.com/dp/B006IVGBDU
Questions
http://www.amazon.com/dp/B006WQ715S
Real Estate Phrases
http://www.amazon.com/dp/B008LQ7BMK
Satisfaction
http://www.amazon.com/dp/B006JM6ING
Selling Air
http://www.amazon.com/dp/B006JOIS5K
SEONemo ThenSEO
http://www.amazon.com/dp/B006JN54LW
SEONemo NowSEO
http://www.amazon.com/dp/B006JMYHYI
SEONemo SoonSEO
http://www.amazon.com/dp/B006JN5606
SMS Mobile Competitions
http://www.amazon.com/dp/B006JO1MLC
SMS Reverse Auction
http://www.amazon.com/dp/B006JOYKI4
Social Media Marketing
http://www.amazon.com/dp/B006Z7VSGW
Stealing You
http://www.amazon.com/dp/B00778TT6E
Surviving A Financial Crisis
http://www.amazon.com/dp/B007J1QH3C
Surviving YOU
http://www.amazon.com/dp/B007J3M6A8
Teen Idols
http://www.amazon.com/dp/B006IWNPYC
The Color of White
http://www.amazon.com/dp/B008GNIOTM

The Complete Health System
http://www.amazon.com/dp/B006IVHG2K
The Denial of Self
http://www.amazon.com/dp/B008B7OK32
The ePubWealth Program
http://www.amazon.com/dp/B008HHHVO6
The Face of Anorexia
http://www.amazon.com/dp/B007F8M4XG
The Face Of Despair
http://www.amazon.com/dp/B006JPOV2S
The Greatest Fraud the World Has Ever Known
http://www.amazon.com/dp/B008GUBKI2
The Missing Link
http://www.amazon.com/dp/B006WQLNTI
The Other Side of Me
http://www.amazon.com/dp/B006JMYAE0
The Pain Game
http://www.amazon.com/dp/B007DIPZX4
The Postcarders
http://www.amazon.com/dp/B006IUUV6O
The Power of Observation
http://www.amazon.com/dp/B006IU99EY
The Psychology of Sales
http://www.amazon.com/dp/B006IUH0GI
The Science of Psychology EXPOSED
http://www.amazon.com/dp/B007JBR682
The Smack Report
http://www.amazon.com/dp/B007AZIELK
The Story of Stupid
http://www.amazon.com/dp/B007L2QCHK
The Truth About Federal Anti-Hoarding Laws
http://www.amazon.com/dp/B007J4KH4O
The Truth About Snow Skiing

http://www.amazon.com/dp/B0072R1SAU
The Vowel Movement
http://www.amazon.com/dp/B0071NUPZY
To Boldly Go Mobile
http://www.amazon.com/dp/B006JNJTEK
Too Late For Fruit; Too Soon For Flowers
http://www.amazon.com/dp/B006IVLXSI
Traffic Jam
http://www.amazon.com/dp/B007SXI0YK
Traffic Media
http://www.amazon.com/dp/B006IUZV28
Video Marketing
http://www.amazon.com/dp/B006XW0J0U
Web Traffic Systems
http://www.amazon.com/dp/B006IVGYAA
What Is It About Yorkies
http://www.amazon.com/dp/B006JMNRQW
Why Men Should Not Be Allowed To Babysit
http://www.amazon.com/dp/B006JMNR6C
Why Women Should Not Use Online Dating Services
http://www.amazon.com/dp/B006J9EMH8
Will I Look Good In This
http://www.amazon.com/dp/B007NCFZ30
Word of Mouth Marketing (WOMM)
http://www.amazon.com/dp/B006X0FXU8
Wordz
http://www.amazon.com/dp/B006IOCSVQ
You Can Run But You Cannot Hide
http://www.amazon.com/dp/B006JLVZC6
You Can't or You Won't
http://www.amazon.com/dp/B007FQ2EJ2

Novels
Common Ground
http://www.amazon.com/dp/B006I5B1YU
Until The Next Time
http://www.amazon.com/dp/B006I7X5JW
No Crimes Beyond Forgiveness
http://www.amazon.com/dp/B006I7WOSA
The Writing of the Wrong
http://www.amazon.com/dp/B006I9FOPI

Religion
BibleBits
http://www.amazon.com/dp/B006ZD702C
Bible Mysteries
http://www.amazon.com/dp/B007J1WZSI
In The Mind of Christ
http://www.amazon.com/dp/B006ZCC8JS
Pastors as Counselors
http://www.amazon.com/dp/B006ZD0I5S
Small Christians
http://www.amazon.com/dp/B008MX216S
The Covenants of the Bible
http://www.amazon.com/dp/B007J3M2GG
The Names of Angels
http://www.amazon.com/dp/B0084S7W9M
The Ten Commitments
http://www.amazon.com/dp/B007LHTR04
Truthful Christianity, Judaism, and Islam
http://www.amazon.com/dp/B007JMIL2G